Perfect Love

— Your Happily Ever After Story —

By

Alice Ebenye

Bola Sobanjo

Cynthia Egbunonu

Eguono Elena Onoyovwi

Esperance M Ntone Epee

Frederique Ndoki

Obaraboye Ine Olude

Olu Sobanjo

Rose Wangechi

ISBN: 978-0-9781595-8-0

DEDICATION

To women all over the world

Join your King in your personal

Happily Ever After Story.

TABLE OF CONTENTS

THANKS

Behind every book is a story of how it came to be. In that story are characters who bring the story to life. And just like the credits that roles at the end of a movie, here is to saying a big thank you to all these wonderful characters as they come into the story. Thank you....

Ade Sobanjo, you may know him as the overall senior pastor of Overcomers worldwide, but I know him first as my best friend, my lover and my pastor. Ade, you are indeed doing a good work pastoring me-your very first member. Thanks for not being tired of my never-ending projects. Thanks for always being a listening ears to me always, thanks for stepping in to cut me some slack as I work hard to finish two books this time around (the other is Weep No More.. you are not forgotten). Thanks for always reading through every sentence to confirm the soundness of my message. You are one in a million and definitely God sent to everyone, me especially.

Demi & Dami, my amazing boys that never stops cheering Mommy on. Thanks for all the hugs and compliments always. Thanks for giving mommy some peace and quite around the house and for praying along for the project. Oh what joy it is each time I hear you called me Mommy. I love you.

To the amazing folks at Grace Press, you make publishing a breeze. Your assistance from inception of this project to completion is highly appreciated. Christ is being honoured through your work. Thanks!

Rose Wangechi Ntone, Obaraboye Ine Olude, Cynthia Egbunonu, Bola Sobanjo, Alice Ebenye, Esperance M Ntone Epee, Frederique Ndoki and last but not least Eguono Elena Onoyovwi, ladies you rock! I am so blessed I have you all in my life. Thanks for not getting mad at me through the drilling process of writing this book, the deadlines, the details, the long emails and more. Thanks for working with God on this with me. I trusted God in each of you to write. I was scared a little bit but I chose to trust God and I must say that you have all confirmed to me over again that you are enjoying this happily ever after life in his perfect love. Now its time to write your own books and do some greater works...are you ready? I am!

Olowo Girls, my amazing blood sisters, sisters in law and nieces. I needed help to enter into women's heads all over the world. I wanted a list of fear that they face and my amazing sisters supplied more than I had enough room for in this book. You all are amazing. I pray that God's love will be made perfect in you.

Other amazing people that helped my contributors. People like Lady Derikoma, who helped co-authored the chapter on Mothers' Love with her daughter Ine, Gbolahan Olude and Sir Wilberforce I. Derikoma for their support to Ine, Clarisse Acho Tinda who co-authored the chapter on God's Unconditional Love with Frederigue and prayerfully supported her through the process, Wambui Kiyanjui, who helped Rose Edit her chapter on the Perfect Love of Christ and Pastor Jean Yves Ntone for his support and inputs for Rose and for his support for Alice on her chapter, Martine Uwamugabe, who edited Eguono's piece on My Ephesians 5 Man. And many others that are not documented here. Thanks!

To the other ladies in Overcomers' (worldwide) that I continue to grow with. Those that would have loved to be on this project but for some reasons could not make it this time. I love you. More to come.

To all staffs and associates at Overcomers, Afropages Magazine and many others that took work off my table during this busy period and those who worked hard to get the book ready. My amazing sister in law, Funmi Sobanjo for your support and encouragement through the process. thanks!

To my friends, family, clients and audience all over the world that are always excited to be a part of what God is doing through me. Thanks!

To the one who loves me with an everlasting love, made me who I am, led me to carry out this project and gave the grace needed all through from A to Z; Thanks Lord!

As I concluded this work and saw all the details of God's mighty hand through the project, I have developed a new love for Charles Jenkins' song My God is Awesome. I cannot stop to sing it and I praise my God forever.

No doubt…my God is REAL!

.†.

PREFACE

Search me, O God, and know my heart; test me and know my anxious thoughts. Point out anything in me that offends you, and lead me along the path of everlasting life. (NLT)

Probe me, God, know my heart; try me, know my thoughts. See if there is a wicked path in me; lead me along an ancient path (MSG)

Search me [thoroughly], O God, and know my heart! Try me and know my thoughts!

And see if there is any wicked or hurtful way in me, and lead me in the way everlasting (AMP)

Psalm 139: 23-24

.†.

INTRODUCTION

It was about 10 years ago; at Rina's wedding. The couple was blessed with a beautiful summer day, fragrances of summer was everywhere. It was a beautiful wedding. The bride looked breathtakingly beautiful, her groom could not stop staring. You could tell how excited both families were to see their children tie the knot. The event was such a lovely one all together. However, I could hardly hear anything they were saying. I only figured out where on the wedding program, after all it's a wedding. You see the issue was that the program was carried out in two languages of which I had little or no understanding - Malagasy and French.

It was a good event and I still enjoyed just watching them and seeing the difference in culture. My husband and I had been invited to the wedding; we had been married for about 2 years at the time. Meanwhile, I love attending weddings. To remember the beautiful day I got married. Funny though, I enjoy other people's wedding more than I did mine. Why? Because on my wedding day I was tensed. I had a plan and I wanted everything to turn out as planned - beautiful. Though Bukky, my amazing wedding planner was in charge, I was still tensed because the perfectionist side of me was still very much alive in 2004.

Anyway, back to Rina's wedding, my darling husband and I would tell each other to sit or stand as we guessed what was going on until we sat for the sermon. I had the wedding pamphlet in my hands and must have been going through the pages to read in French when I felt an arm around me. I was so sure it was Ade's arms. Felt warm and reassuring but then I looked to the side and saw both of his arms on his laps. Wow! That was when I realized that my darling father was trying to tell me something.

The story before that is that prior to this particular day, I had recently started questioning God love for me. I was not really convinced that I really matter to anyone including God. I remember that we had a meeting at our apartment on Cranbrooke Avenue (in Montreal) a few Saturdays before Rina's wedding and that I led a song that goes like this:

> I want to know you
>
> I want to see your face
>
> I want to know you more
>
> I want to touch you
>
> I want to hear your voice
>
> I want to know you more

And immediately after that meeting I said the opposite to God in my heart: "I don't want to know you, I want you to know me. No one in this world understands me, people I meet actually care about themselves, their own need and desires, no one cares enough to take time to know me, but rather they all want life to be about them.

If you ask me what exactly was really wrong at the time, I don't remember, did someone hurt me? Was someone mad at me? I really don't remember what exact incidence increased my life's frustration at the time but I simply remember that I was feeling frustrated and overwhelmed.

And so I thought in my heart that God was the same, though he may be a bit better, he also is a leader that I would call a dictator God. He has a plan and would not care whether I like it or not, He wants me to be just what he wants. Do you see why I was saying to God that I didn't want to know him? I would rather want him to take some time to know me, to discover what I loved to do, to understand what I don't enjoy, to accept me for who I am. As I look back now I laugh, how easily emotion consumes us that lies become so real to us more than the truth.

Anyway, flash forward now to Rina's wedding, and the mysterious arms that I felt around me, I asked Ade if he had just put his arms around me he also confirmed that he didn't. I felt God saying to me, I love you. Oh! How overwhelming it was. God said to me, you funny girl! You actually want to tell me who you are and what you like or don't like, have you forgotten that I made you? I formed you and designed. Your personality, your talents, your capacity, and your abilities, I packaged them the way they are. I made you to glorify me and guess what? I know you more than you know or can ever know yourself".

Wow! What an amazing revelation it was for me. And that, my dear reader, was where my discovery began. That was about the time that my Happily Ever after story began, when I began to desire to know more about this so called heavenly Father. Each time I remember that time in my life, I marvel at the way God dealt with the whole situation. Mind you, I had given my life to Christ many years prior to this event, I had taught in the Church and risen to the position of leadership in many occasions and I had also made some mistakes I never thought were possible in my books. I taught in churches and ministered in many capacities. However it was only at this time that I began to understand God's love for me. According to our main text in this book, God's love had not been made perfect in me, though I thought I was saved prior to this incidence, there is the possibility that I was not. And you will see as we go along as he shows us how to know whether we are saved or not.

In this book I want to expose to you what the love of God is for you my dear reader. If you already know him, great! You will still gain more but if you don't, I want to get you to a place where you will fully discover what you already have in the one who loved you.

Over the last couple of years as I have really known the true love of God and continue to do so, God has brought some amazing ladies my way, those that we have grown together with. Those I have shared God with, had opportunity of hearing their stories, guided them and continue to, ladies that I have seen transform as I continue to as well. I have invited some of these ladies to share of what they know of Gods love with you and their input has formed a beautiful addition to the precious book in your hands. And I am happy to say that you will be learning from a bunch of ladies that would not only say it but will do what the word says because they know God's love for them.

Our main scriptural focus will be on John's account of God's love as written in:

> *1 John 4: 18. There is no fear in love; but perfect love casts out fear: because fear hath torment. He that fear is not made perfect in love. (KJV)*

In all, I am sure that this book will tremendously bless you

.†.

NO ROOM

As far back as I can remember, fear has been a major emotion that I have dealt with and still do. However John is saying with confidence in this our text that if I have fear it is a sign that God's love has not yet being made perfect in me

1 John 4: 18. There is no fear in love; but perfect love casts out fear: because fear hath torment. He that fears has not been made perfect in love. (KJV)

I don't know about you, but this makes me want to investigate further. To start, lets take a moment to get some background information about John. What gives him the right to make such declarations? John is the same that was one of Jesus' first few disciples; he was among Jesus' inner circle (Peter, James and John). It was the mother of James and John that came to Jesus asking him to make her sons be on his right and left arms at his kingdom in heaven (Matthew 20:20), He walked with Jesus almost all through our Lord's mission on earth. He wrote 5 books in the New Testament: John's Gospel, 1st 2nd & 3rd John and Revelation. He was the same one that later suffered for Christ and was banished to the island of Patmos where he saw the details in a vision as recorded in the book of Revelation (Matthew 20:22, Mark 10: 38-39).

In John 21:20. John, while writing an account of what happened while Jesus was on earth, and needed to describe himself said "Peter turned and saw the <u>disciple whom Jesus loved</u> following them, the one who also had leaned back against him during the supper and had said, "Lord, who is it that is going to betray you?" When you read through his writings you will notice a theme of love. He experienced God's love and took it upon himself to share that with us. He also wrote down the very popular John 3:16 For God so loved the world, that he gave his one and only son, that whosoever believes in him should not perish but have everlasting life.

It was this same John whom Jesus was talking to at the cross about his mother.

John 19: 25-27

Now there stood by the cross of Jesus his mother, and his mother's sister, Mary the wife of Cleophas, and Mary Magdalene. When Jesus therefore saw his mother, and the disciple standing by, whom he loved, he said to his mother, Woman, behold thy son! Then He said to the disciple, Behold your mother! And from that hour that disciple took her unto his own home.

From the records, we see that not only did John claim to be loved by Jesus but that Jesus really did love him. At least when Jesus was leaving the earth the only person He entrusted his precious mother to was our dear brother John. From all this we can agree that John qualifies to share what he shared in all his writings. And we can actually agree that he is someone to listen to.

Therefore when he says there is no room for fear in Love we must pay close attention to what he says. There is no room for fear in Love. New Living Translation says it this way: Such Love has no fear, because perfect love expels all fear John was trying to describe the love of God for his readers. So many truths to note in this verse:

- First that there are different kinds of love, perfect and I guess imperfect. And we will look at love in closer details in a later chapter.
- Second is that in God's perfect love there is no room for fear,
- Third that since fear has torment, anyone that has fear dominating them has not been fully perfected in this perfect love,

- Fourth when one receives God's perfect love, it dispels all fear.

To proceed I would love us to first consider what fear is. In Greek, (the language that John wrote in originally) the word translated to fear in this verse is 'Phobo'. The Origin of Phobia.

Fear, according to the Merriam-Webster Dictionary, is defined in the following ways:

: to be afraid of something or someone

: to expect or worry about something bad or unpleasant

: to be afraid and worried.

Fear is an upsetting negative sensation brought about by a perceived threat. It is no doubt a basic survival mechanism employed as a response to a particular stimulus, like threat of danger or pain. Fear produces two responses: the urge to flee or confront the situation otherwise known as the fight-or-flight response. In severe and excessive cases of fear like terror and horror, the victims are paralyzed or freeze to the spot.

What is the foundation of fear? Fear can be explained in very many ways.

1. Fear as the misplacement of truth.

If you have ever being afraid of the dark as a little child you will agree with me on this point. A little girl is in bed, lights out and its time to sleep but the image formed on the wall sends messages to her mind. What is that? She can't look for fear of actually discovering that a monster is actually in her room with her. She may even scream for help to be delivered from this monster. But is it a real monster? No just some tree outside her room casting its shadows into our little angel's room. However, though the truth is that it's not a real monster, she is scared to death that this monster might hurt her. Is that true? When the truth is misplaced fear develops and many suffer and even perish when its only a shadow of the truth.

2. Fear as an anxiety gap between the now and the future.

When you are in the present and your mind wonders to know what might happened in the future.

This process of wondering begins to communicate with your mind and the sends messages to the brain to form different emotions. Even though the messages that your mind creates and communicates may not be true, the body does not think that way but acts as though they are real. Worries become real the more the thought goes on, and soon develops into a theory that determines what we do or not.

3. Fear as a protective emotion.

Fear helps you to react or not when faced with dangerous animals or situations. This kind of fear is the kind that is learnt, a universal emotion; pre-programed into all people and animal as a way of instinctively responding to potential danger. This kind is an adaptive behavior that we possess to help us recognize threats. It is a capability that has made it possible for us as humans to survive natural disasters and predators. All persons unconsciously or consciously experience some sort of fear one time or another. That is why you see some in some part of the world afraid of spiders because the spiders around them are not simple spiders but toxic and the same set of people not afraid in a bit of huge snakes because there are non-poisonous snakes around them. On the other hand some others in another part of the world are not moved when they see spider but the can't stand snakes. This kind of fear is a defense mechanism for adaptation. It is somewhat normal to have this kind of fear but when it is focused upon to the extreme it becomes a snare to the person. It can keep a person indoors for months, scared that something bad may happen to them.

4. Fear as respect for God.

This kind of fear is very different from the others. You will see it stated in various books of the bible. This fear is described as the respect a man has for the sovereign God. This fear helps a person to recognize God for who he is. It helps us regard God correctly and so we are also able to recognize ourselves correctly with reference to God. The fear of the Lord helps us to see God as the All knowing, almighty, all wise, holy, and righteous God and that way we are able to humble ourselves before him.

John says, that when God's love has been made perfect in you, it leaves no room for fear. In the next chapter we will take a look at fear and its torments.

.†.

FEAR HAS TORMENT

Pay close attention to this phrase: fear has torment! How true is that? Have you ever been overtaken by fear? This reminds me of a particular day recently. I was fast asleep. And in my dreams I saw an armed robber at my window in the middle of the night. He was instructing me to open the door forcefully. I woke up in terror and was so scared. I was sweating and really full of anxieties. You see I live in Nigeria as I write this book and we hear other people's experiences with armed robbers and all that came flashing back to my mind. On this particular night I could no longer continue my sleep. I tried to pray but I could not wave off the terror. I had to wake my husband up to pray with me. It was only after he prayed with me that I was able to go back to sleep. Thank God he was around. When someone is overwhelmed by fear it becomes a torment for such persons. Fear then can also be explained as something as strong as faith but in the negative. You believe something so strongly and that believe makes you to act in fear.

If Faith, according to Hebrews 11:1 is the assurance of things hoped for, the evidence of things not seen. Therefore Fear is also the reaction based on what is perceived from situations that causes its victim to respond according to their perception. Fear tend to shape a response that may seem exaggerated, but nonetheless realistic to the person. Such responses are emotional and can generally be altered when substantial evidence is presented that the situation feared most does not pose an immediate threat.

Here is a list of the fear that we face on a daily basis or over a lifetime:

1. Fear of the unknown
2. Fear of getting hurt
3. Fear of attempting to move forward
4. Fear of trusting others
5. Fear of trusting God
6. Fear of losing loved ones
7. Fear of hell
8. Fear of raising ungodly children
9. Fear of accidents
10. Fear of not meeting deadlines
11. Fear of getting old
12. Fear of taking a wrong step
13. Fear of wrong investments
14. Fear of the future
15. Fear of taking risks
16. Fear of the dark
17. Fear of loosing control
18. Fear of not aging gracefully
19. Fear of being neglected by loved ones

20. Fear of not being valued
21. Fear of not being understood
22. Fear of loosing properties
23. Fear of loosing one's dignity
24. Fear of not finding a nice partner
25. Fear of being lonely
26. Fear of not being accepted
27. Fear of Losing a child
28. Fear of divorce
29. Fear of disease like breast cancer
30. Fear of weight gain/loss
31. Fear of no longer being attractive
32. Fear of heart disease
33. Fear of being left alone in old age
34. Fear of social situations
35. Fear of change (environment, marital status, physical health etc.)
36. Fear of identity theft.
37. Fear of people
38. Fear of being excluded
39. Fear of not having a say
40. Fear of poverty

41. Fear of being too rich
42. Fear of losing access to what we already have
43. Fear of being back stabbed
44. Fear of being judged by others
45. Fear of height
46. Fear of unanswered prayers
47. Fear of not getting one's rights

Fear can originate from our past personal experiences and even from the experiences of others. Our brain senses a similarity in the situation and that triggers an emotion within us that renders us useless for the time period. All these fears except the fear of God evaporates the more of God's love we know and the more the fear of God increases in us.

Many people's behavior is as a result of their fear. Fear is major factor that has shaped the world the way it is today. Wars and offences have their roots in fear.

As I have recently studied this topic of perfect love, I have read many stories in the bible and have seen the fear behind many actions especially in women. Here are a few:

Fear of Restriction: Eve

I always wonder why Satan approached Eve first and not Adam. Could it be because he thought if He gets the woman down it would be easy for her to get her husband down? Probably! Anyway, from that story of the fall, Eve's behaviour was as a result of the fear she already had, the devil only preyed on that. Satan was questioning how satisfied or contented Eve was with her new world and life by his question in:

> **Genesis 3: 2** *"Has God indeed said, 'You shall not eat of every tree of the garden'?" NKJV*

He was trying to sense how satisfied she was with the limitations she had in the garden. How could she be happy if she was restricted from one of the trees in the garden? Satan saw this fear of being limited as an opportunity and used it against Eve. He diverted her attention from the myriad of things that God had done to the only limitation she had, showed her some outcomes of the fear (you can not be like God if you don't eat the fruit) and easily got her to yield to doing something against the will of her wonderful Lord that has given her everything else. This resulted in the fall of man (human).

Isn't it the same with us today?

Fear of Unfulfilled Promises: Sarah

It was fear that moved Sarah to give her hand maiden to her husband to marry.

Genesis 16:

Now Sarai Abram's wife had borne him no children. And she had an Egyptian maidservant, whose name was Hagar. So Sarai said to Abram, 'See now, the Lord has restrained me from bearing children. Please, go in to my maid; perhaps I shall obtain children by her. And Abram hearkened to the voice of Sarai

Sarah here (still Sarai before her name changed to Sarah) got tired of waiting for God and so decided to help God since he was too slow for her. Her fears led her to do something she later regretted, something that cause pain to her and her children's children.

Fear of Injustice: Tamar

Tamar was the widow of Judah's son, Er. The law in Israel at the time was that if a man dies without a son the brother should help propagate his lineage so that the child born then would be the one to receive the late man's inheritance and also care for the widow in her older years. The next in line that was supposed to help also died; he wasn't willing to help produce a child for his brother. Tamar was moved by the fear of not having a child to take care of her and help carry on the lineage of her late husband.

At that time in Israel, the woman's most important role is to bring forth children. Tamar was moved by fear of being seen as useless to sin. She pretended to be a prostitute and seduced her father in law. Thereby bringing forth a child to continue the lineage, even the lineage of Christ. The story ended well, adding Tamar to the same lineage that Christ came from. However this doesn't mean that God encourages prostitution. It only means that God's mercy is also available for the prostitute. We see this clearly in the story of the woman that was caught in adultery and brought to be stoned where Jesus was. His mercy washed her and He said to her go and sin no more.

Fear of Loneliness and Destruction: Bathsheba

2 Samuel 11 records how David saw Bathsheba having a bath and was tempted. He sent for Bathsheba and She on the other hand must have missed her own husband who had been at war for a while. Was is it her fear of loneliness that moved her to have a bath where she could possibly be seen by others? We don't know. However, we can say that either her fears of being destroyed by the king or of continuing in her loneliness weakened her strength to say no

to David. She got pregnant and eventually this led to the execution of her husband, Uriah.

Fear for sure has torment. Its that same fear that affected the woman at the well.

Fear of Being Looked down on: Samaritan Woman

The woman that had an encounter with Jesus at the well in Sicah must have decided to go fetch water in the sun, when others would have gone in the morning. Her life was not like that of the normal women in her village that had one husband and their own children. It was opposite, she had been with many men and wasn't even legally married to the person she was with at the time. She preferred to be alone in order to avoid having to answer some 'unnecessary' question from nosy people. She would rather face the heat of the sun than the shame of being ridiculed.

Thankfully, Christ knew her and what His visit would mean to her. And because of that Christ had to make a quick stop to launch her into her very own happily ever after life. He went through her city on his way to Galilee, broke all odds to get His perfect love across to her. She received

Christ's life and went everywhere telling others about Jesus.

> *John incidentally also recorded this story in John 4: 1-26*

This woman and many others have had their stories transformed by the perfect love of Christ. In my own life, Christ has made a huge difference and in the lives of many other ladies that I have either read about or come in contact with.

Some of my own personal friends have been invited to contribute to this book by writing about their own view of this perfect love. Enjoy God's truth according to them and I will see you in the final chapter.

Consider our text again:

> *1 John 4: 18. There is no fear in love; but perfect love casts out fear, because fear involves torment. But he who fears has not been made perfect in love. (NKJV)*

.†.

God's Love is Unconditional

By Frederique Ndoki

I am the beloved of God and He has a perfect plan for my life. His love for me does not depend on my past, present, works, feelings or emotions. He doesn't love me because I am lovable or love Him back. He loves me simply because He is love.

Isn't it wonderful to declare this? How much richer will our lives be when we know it, believe it, live it and ultimately experience this amazing love. This is what this chapter is all about. To truly understand what the unconditional love of God towards us means. So where do we begin this love story? Let's start by looking at the Biblical definition of God's love.

The meaning of love

1 John 4:9-10:"In this the love of God was manifested toward us, that God has sent His only begotten Son into the world, that we might live through Him. In this is love, not that we loved God, but that He Loved us and sent His Son to be the propitiation for our sins."

As you can see in these verses, God loved us so much that He gave to us His most precious gift, His Son Jesus Christ, in order that we can be saved from eternal judgment (Joel 3: 11 -17). The kind of love He shows us is unconditional, meaning it does not depend on us, but is manifested because He loved us first even when we were separated from Him. It is clear therefore that we are talking about a sacrificial love, committed to the wellbeing of the other. This is the God kind of love; known as agape. 1 Corinth 13:4-8 provides more detail to this definition: "Love is patient, love is kind, it is not jealous;

love does not brag and is not arrogant, does not act unbecomingly; it does not seek its own, is not provoked, does not take into account a wrong suffered, does not rejoice in unrighteousness, but rejoices with the truth; bears all things, believes all things, hopes all things and endures all things. Love never fails." This is why the Bible describes love as the greatest gift of all.

To whom is God's Love directed:

God's love is therefore destined towards all of His creation. It is His desire that no one should perish but that all will repent in order to experience eternal life with the Father (2Peter: 3:9). You are therefore included and personally touched by this love. This has always been the original plan; executed to perfection since the beginning of creation to Satan's biggest consternation. This love manifested in the person of Jesus Christ, gives the assurance that He loves each of us individually.

Does this mean that God loves us equally?

Have you ever wondered if God loves every person equally? Can His love be personal, directed specially and specifically to each individual, yet equally to every one of His creation? The answer to this question is yes. Equality here means that He does not love one person more or less than another. His love is not measurable. It signifies however, that His Love for you and I is intimate and unique; and seeks just one thing, which is the salvation of your soul (2 Corinth 5: 17-21). He is ready to abandon everything else without hesitation and come in search of you alone; intervening in your favor, rejoicing greatly when he has found you, as seen in the parable of the lost sheep (Luke 15: 4-7).

Why does the devil try so hard to destroy our perception of God's love?

As a child of God, you need to understand one thing very clearly. There is someone after your life. Satan is not sitting by idly. The Bible is clear about this. 1 Peter 5:8 warns that "Your adversary, *(enemy)* the devil is prowling about like a roaring lion, seeking whom to devour *(destroy).*" Here is the enemy whose sole mission is to turn you away from your creator. He has at his disposition all kinds of ruses and tricks to weaken you mentally and instill doubt in you. He attacks your thoughts, making it difficult for you to believe what God says about you. No wonder we are admonished severally to be of sober spirit and to constantly renew our minds on the Word of God. God's plans for us are of peace, to give us a future and a hope. (Jeremiah 29:11). He has prepared good things for us (Eph.2:10).

Why therefore does it seem so easy to believe Satan's lies even when the Lord asks us to submit to Him and to resist the devil so that he can flee from us?(James 4:7) It is simply because we have let ourselves to be governed by the flesh for too long. And we know that the flesh takes pleasure in obeying the lies of the devil. To fully experience the love of God, the time has come for us to completely believe God's promises concerning us. You should know therefore that a solid faith in God's love and Word, are the tools for defeating the devil. This is why the apostle Paul in Romans 8: 39 reassures us that: "For I am convinced that neither death, nor life, nor angels, nor principalities, nor things present, nor things to come, nor powers, nor height, nor depth, nor any other created thing, will be able to separate us from the love of God, which is in Christ Jesus our Lord."

Does God love me even when I do not feel his love? Does God love me despite my past or even my present circumstances?

God loves you whether you feel it or not and His love is not dependent upon your emotions, or feelings. He loved you first and His love lasts eternally. His love does not depend on your past or present circumstances (John 9:1-4); nor on the fact that you do not live according to His Word (John 8:4-11). He loves you and longs for an intimate relationship with you.

So why do you sometimes still have doubts and guilt; feelings that that make you think that God loves you less or not at all? This is because the devil tries to instill these doubts and fears in your mind making you believe that you are unworthy of God's love. It may be as a result of the type of lifestyle you are living or that you do not fully understand the inheritance you have in Christ Jesus.

To experience the fullness of His love you need to accept Jesus as your Lord and Savior through repentance and confession of sin. For whoever confesses Jesus Christ as the Son of God and Savior of the world, is forgiven of their sins. God abides in Him, and he in God (1John4:15-19). You have been made perfect in the love of the Father. You need to understand that the lies and doubts of the devil, therefore no longer have any power over you because the perfect love of Christ casts out all fear. You are now able to love Him too, because He loved you first.

There is no need to be afraid or be condemned by the guilt of your past sins. At the cross, Jesus Christ offered salvation even to the condemned thief telling him: "Assuredly, I say to you, today you will be with Me in paradise" (Luke 23:43). The psalmist declares in Psalm 23:4-5: "Yea, though I walk through the valley of the shadow of death, I will fear no evil; for you are with me, your rod and your staff they comfort me. You prepare a table before me in the presence of my enemies; you anoint my head with oil; my cup runs over."

In your walk with the Lord, have the complete assurance that His plans for you are good; to prosper you and not to harm you, to give you a hope and a future. Confess His promises about your life because you become what you confess. You will come to the understanding that His love for you is not influenced by anything. He simply loves you! You did not have to pay for it. He loved you so much that He gave you the greatest gift in the person of Christ Jesus.

In a nut shell

I conclude this chapter with a testimony of the manifestation of the true love and power of God at work. When I was asked to participate in this project, even though I thought it was a fantastic idea, I almost turned down the opportunity because my first language is not English. How was I going to write a whole chapter in a language that I was not very comfortable with? However, I had a strong conviction from the Holy Spirit not to exclude myself and to work closely with a specific sister, who would help me conquer the language barrier.

Before beginning the writing process, we spent some time in prayer declaring specifically that through the Holy Spirit, this book will have a huge impact on the lives of young women. While we were working and developing points about God's unconditional love towards us, we heard a sudden noise as if someone had fallen, coming from the other room of the house. Knowing that another sister was with us at home, we went to verify what was happening. We found her on the floor groaning, seemingly being attacked by a contrary spirit. After praying with and for her, she testified that while she heard us talking about the unconditional love of Christ, she began to feel a sudden and violent anger towards us; and did not want to stay in the house anymore. She tried to leave by the back door in order not to hear the discussion, but something pulled her back inside.

This was a confirmation of one of the points elaborated on earlier. Isn't it amazing how angry the devil becomes when we receive the true revelation of the love of God towards us. The enemy will do everything in his power to blind us and prevent us from walking in the fullness of God's unconditional love. My prayer for every reader of this book is to experience the full revelation of this powerful love of Christ. It is for this reason that we should never stop proclaiming it to everyone around us; a love that brings freedom and deliverance. The Bible says that we will know the truth and the truth shall set us free. This was exactly the case with our sister. She was able to experience the love of Christ in a whole new dimension.

Frederique Ndoki is from Douala, Cameroon and the third child in a family of four sisters. Born and brought up in a religious environment; giving her the foundations of Christian education which eventually enabled her to surrender her life to Christ in her adolescence.

She is trained as an IT Technician but currently works in the banking sector. Due to studies, she got the opportunity to travel to several countries, experiencing different cultures and meeting Christians from all walks of life. These experiences contributed to making her the person she is today; desiring more than ever to serve the Living God, Creator of the universe, her Saviour and first Love. She is passionate about spreading the Gospel in order to enable everyone understand that Christ loves them and that His love is unchanging and without limits.

.†.

The Power Of God's Love

By Alice Ebenye

1 John 4: 16

And we have known and believed the love that God has for us. God is love, and he who abides in love abides in God, and God in him.

God is Love

He created us out of love and His love is infinite. However, we must know and believe this truth.

An Error?

Ooops! This is what is often said when a mistake when performing an act which we do not wish the consequences, what a mistake is commonly called. For a long time I thought I was a mistake; I thought nobody liked me or did not want me.

I was the girl who thought she was a mistake, the result of adultery. Though that is not a big deal in our world today.... unfortunately.

Well, when you think you were an error, it's hard to love and be loved. It is difficult to believe that God loves us and definitely hard to receive and accept his love. And since I lived away from my nuclear family and my biological father had not recognized me; I agreed that I was a mistake for sure. Funny as it may seem, it was easier to believe the lies of the enemy. But thank God what Satan wanted to destroy, God has patiently rebuilt with love.

With the love of God I realized that before I was born, He had already desired my existence, he had carefully chosen me and created me. He had a plan for my life, a destiny. What a comfort!

Jeremiah 1: 5

Jeremiah 29: 11

A Crazy decision...A crazy choice!

John 3: 16

> *For God so loved the world that He gave His only begotten Son, that whoever believes in Him should not perish but have everlasting life.*

"I'm sure that in your entire life you may never have heard of another person that took such a decision, it may seem foolish, I concede! "Who does that? "Will we say, in a tone sarcastic and mockingly. No one sees the danger and run to it, nobody sees death and kisses it. Hello?? !! Who does this kind of thing?

Well! Such a person did exist! Yes a "crazy one" shall we say, who against all odds, braved the obstacles. One who saw death and walked right to it, impetuously, like a conqueror.

Of course, we have wonderful examples of people who have dedicated their lives to their peers, however, whether it is the external or inner changes do not change their destiny on earth, which in short is honorable and not bad considering the individualistic world we live in.

However, my heart is still pounds when I hear a song I really love that says, "I have loved you even before you will know what love was. I saw everything, yet I chose the cross" (Steffani Gretzinger: Out of the Hiding, The undoing)

He chose the cross, despite the corruption of my heart, despite my choice to hazardous and harmful consequences. He chose the cross for me, by love, despite the lack of love in my heart, for my fellow men, he chose the cross although I was living a life of disobedience, (feeling intoxicating at times) despite ... We could put so many things after this "despite" He saw EVERYTHING (past, present and future) and nothing frightened him. He persevered in his choice of unmistakable and imperturbable way, a hero!

He did not retreat from my sexual choices; it did not retreat from my wickedness and my lack of love. He did not back off from my laziness, he did not shrink that my thoughts were against His principles. These are not obstacles that lacked the course, neither fewer thorns nor the nails on the cross. He chose to love despite all these obstacles from the best to the worst. Who makes this kind of choices, tell me? " A mad person! "

Yes mad love! A fiery love! He loves me so much that He left everything for me. He gave his life, he loves me enough to correct me, take me back each time, to bring me back on track, to feed me, protect me, forgive me, even more than a mother it is for me at all times. When I was going through the darkest moments of my life, he was, tirelessly drying my tears, putting each piece of my heart back to the place it belongs, with the patience it take to put the 15,000 pieces puzzle or more together, year after year.

So the question I ask is: who would not love such a person? Who?

What crazy one would make the mistake of ignoring this wonderful person? Who will take the risk of ignoring this avalanche of love? This tsunami of love? Who would take that stupid decision?

Believe me I've made some decisions not very smart then this I did will not be one of them!

Not me !

John 15: 16

Who am I? Another...

Some people have an aura that makes you notice them; others call it charisma or presence. Well its presence cannot remain unnoticed. It is love, you cannot switch to side as it will, it permeates you, transforms you.

Indeed, when we start a friendship with someone, spend time together with someone we begin to have similar values and our habits begin to become similar. We see that we are different from what we were before our friendship and that we start to look alike.

I experienced the same thing when my relationship with Jesus began, It was like I no longer recognize myself and began to notice the changes made in me, my personality, and my way of thinking, my perspectives, the way I talked to people, all of it changed. I remember, I used to chose people to love according to criteria of beauty, clothing or just those who had the same thinking as me. What the love of God does in our lives is this: a profound transformation, a change in value, change of priority.

2 Corinthians 17

Patience

Recently, I went to the emergency room and I wondered for the umpteenth time why hospitals customers were called patients. And I see you smiling (as yo read that); they are actually sitting patiently in waiting rooms for hours and hours to be received by the doctor or nurse. I reiterated it to myself for the umpteenth time.

My definition of patient however takes a whole other dimension when I think of my creator, the aspect of love comes into its own, so for me patience is love.

In my case, until my eyes opened and I recognized the presence of God's greatness and submitting my life to Him has taken many years, He put different people on my path to teach me his word, share with me his love. He let me go through all kinds of trials of my choice (the ones I mentioned above and more) but patiently He knocked incessantly, tirelessly with love.

Until the day my heart stopped being hardening, my heart has received desperate love.

What is surprising is that he never gave up, never. He faced a tremendous amount of obstacles, indifference, stubbornness, my ignorance and I even abandonment him many times but he did not give up, He persevered ... fortunately for me, you…

I have never been so at peace, as happy as when He came into my life with His unconditional and unwavering love.

This love is real, powerful, it transforms and renews everything and above all is patient, do not let it pass you by, you will not find another of this kind.

Real happiness is well and truly close to you and not in the meadow! Can you hear Him say: I love you?

Yes? Seize the opportunity to be loved as never before and privileged to love in return.

1 Corinthians 13: 4

Alice Ebenye is a graduate in International Business and has been a professional in the banking industry for about 9 years.

She has been attending Overcomers Assembly for almost 10 years. Previously, Alice was in charge of the Children Ministry for the same numbers of years and she coordinates the Reception and welfare department at Overcomers Assembly. She is welcoming and enjoy meeting new people.

She is dedicated to walking and growing in her relationship with God and also help others do the same as she leads 'Love God first' one of the life groups at Overcomers Assembly.

.†.

The Perfect Love of Christ

By Rose Wangechi

When Pastor Olu asked me if I would be willing to contribute a chapter to this book, I was humbled by the opportunity but afraid of the responsibility that had been bestowed upon me. The weight of writing about a subject as complex as love was simply daunting. While praying, I was reminded of a very unique love story in the book of John, chapter 11. It's a story that illuminates love and, exemplifies the perfect love of Christ in a manner that is relatable to women even today. It reveals a love deeply rooted in trust, and dependence on the power of God. It demonstrates a unique friendship between Christ and two sisters who were inherently different (in their approach to the gospel) but similar in their understanding of the love of Christ.

The Miriam Webster dictionary defines love as "an unselfish loyal and benevolent concern for the good of another" or as; "the fatherly concern of God for humankind". In both of these explanations, we see that love can only exist where there is a "concern", either from one man to another, or, from God to man, and/or vice-versa.

It is in the context of love as the "fatherly concern of God for humankind" that we shall examine and elucidate the love of Christ, as demonstrated by His relationship with the two sisters, Mary and Martha as described in chapter 11 of the book of John. The bible records that one day, a man named Lazarus who lived in a village called Bethany, fell sick and died. His sisters—Mary and Martha, sent a message to Jesus saying; *"Lord, whom You love (so well) is sic*k". (John 11: 3, AMP). These words reveal a sincere cry to a trusted friend. They reveal a personal connection between Jesus and the siblings. They bring to life a human connection that we can relate to in our own relationships with Christ.

When in trouble, people tend to go to or call on people they trust. When asked to provide an emergency contact at the hospital, at school, or the workplace, most people will give a number of someone they are related to—one they deem loyal, trustworthy and dependable. In most cases, we only give out the number of a close family member or friend, someone with whom, we have an established bond. In other words, we go for someone, to whom we are certain of his/her love and care. We wholly depend and trust that should there be an emergency, the person will show up without fail. By looking at Mary and Martha's message to Jesus, we can sense a similar kind of trust based bond. They believed that Jesus loved them dearly. In fact, the bible reaffirms that bond in verse 5 which says; "*Now Jesus loved Martha and her sister and Lazarus. (They were his dear friends, and He Held them in loving esteem)* (John 11: 5, AMP).

Does that kind of a relationship apply to us, to-day? Do we believe that Jesus holds us in high esteem, as He did Lazarus, Mary and Martha? We have assurance of this as the bible tells us that God does not change. (James 1:17) He is eternal and His words and promises never change! As such, we can we afford to believe and proclaim, that Jesus loves us, and He holds us in high esteem. It's a bold statement that must come from women after God's heart, with our own hearts rooted in faith and understanding that Jesus Christ is trustworthy, and dependable. We must dare to believe in such a relationship through the lenses of trust.

I believe that Martha and Mary trusted in that kind of perfect love. They relied on their conviction that Jesus loved them, and Lazarus enough. He cared for them. The bible says that; *When Martha heard that Jesus was coming, she went to meet him...Martha then said to Jesus, Master, if You had been here, my brother would not have died.* (John 11: 20; AMP). The bible also adds that; *"when Mary came to the place where Jesus was and saw Him, she dropped down at His feet, saying to Him, Lord, if You had been here, my brother would not have died.* (John 11: 32, AMP). When you read their statements, I hope that you can sense their boldness and trust in Christ's love and power. The society today suggests that most women have "trust issues", we are singled out as erratic, and, irrational in our tendency towards mistrust. It is not uncommon to hear pundits in the media argue with zeal that most women do not get appointed in corporate leadership positions because of their mistrust. Contrary to the claims, I believe that women are fundamentally trusting. The experiences some of us have had to deal with causes us to err on the side of caution. Past experiences that are hurtful, or emotionally disturbing may cause any woman (or man) to exhibit a deep sense of fear which, then breeds mistrust. An understanding of the perfect love of Christ and the uniqueness of such a relationship is the only solution capable of dealing with any bad experience of the past, and instead, give rise to a new culture of women who are trusting, and whole. Because the love of Christ brings no fear, it will cause us to face the daily struggles with a confident mentality of 'Jesus cares', and He will always show up to our rescue. When He does, needs will be met, lives will be healed, families will be comforted, chains will be broken, and the dead will be brought to life, and so on.

When Jesus saw Mary sobbing over the loss of her brother Lazarus, the bible records in verse 33, that he was deeply moved in spirit and troubled. Jesus cares about His friends and we are His friends, which means, when we are heart-broken and sad, His spirit is in distress. It's good to know that our pain becomes His pain. When Jesus arrived at Lazarus' house, he asked the people, where they had laid him. The bible records that when He got to the tomb; *"Jesus wept"* (John 11:35, AMP). Out of his compassion and love, Christ wept for Lazarus and He does the same for us today! If we can allow Him to come into our lives; to address the pain and the hurt we are in today, He will come! He raised Lazarus from dead. Surely, He can raise and deliver any woman (or man) who dares to believe in His selfless love, and loyal benevolent concern for

His precious daughters. We are God's vessels of grace, and He is concerned about us. He is willing to meet with us to address our needs and expectations, without delay.

In order for Jesus to access Lazarus, the boulder which, protected his tomb had to be removed. So Jesus ordered it removed, but Martha exclaimed; *" Lord, by this time he is decaying and throws off an offensive odour, for he has been dead for four days".* (John 11: 39; AMP). Martha's response to Christ reminded me of my own answers to Him when He tried to penetrate into my heart in order to deal with some personal struggles and experiences. I just couldn't let Him in. I had an explanation for every question so I consciously and unconsciously kept on redirecting Him in order to save Him the agony of having to deal with my messy past. It's possible to hinder Jesus, like Martha did. When the Holy Spirit paved way for me to see that Jesus couldn't care less about the odour of Lazarus' decaying body. I was truly impressed! Jesus was on a mission to free Lazarus. And He is always on a mission to free His children from bondage. This particular story reminds me of those devoted nurses who sacrifice their comfort, out of love, to care for the sick people. My sister-in-law is one such nurse, and she loves to take care of the sick. She gives patients the best medical care. She desires to help them stay alive--especially those who are in their final stage of life. I can't imagine her saying that she would not help clean a patient because he or she is too smelly! Her compassion outweighs any fear and discomfort on her part. We need not point Jesus away from our wounds. They are not offensive to him. We just need to let Him clean the wound and to bring any dead thing in our lives back to life.

His Perfect love will always bring the freedom and relief similar to Lazarus, Martha and Mary's. At the end of this beautiful story, the bible points to Jesus of Nazareth, asking the people to "free Lazarus". He ordered the burial wrappings around him removed! Once Christ has entered into our hearts, and into our lives, He will unshackle every chain of bondage. He will set you free! I find the gesture of “unwrapping the burial wrappings” quite symbolic and relevant to us today because physically, Lazarus was alive but he could not move because he was physically bound! It's possible for us to be free yet imprisoned. If the Lord forgives, we ought to be free! If that conviction does not sink and settle in our hearts, we shall remain chained by our own unforgiving spirit. Our own inability to focus on the completed work of the Cross can hinder our progress and delay our testimonies. We can be born again Christians who are shackled by the things of the past or present. We can be shackled in our minds!

It is my prayer that as you read this book, you'll find it in your heart to trust the Lord, and to allow Him through the power of the Holy Spirit, to point you to the areas of your life, that you could be still bound by the devil. I believe that once Jesus has set you free, nobody, or nothing should hold you captive! Christ desires the best out of your life.

And that's why, He said to Martha that; *"did I not tell you and promise you that if you believe and rely on Me, you will see the glory of God?"* (John 11: 40, AMP).

I encourage you to believe in Christ and His promises, and you shall, surely see the glory of God in your own life.

Rose Wangechi is a native of Kenya. She is currently a graduate student of Northeastern University where she is pursuing a Master of Science degree in Nonprofit Management, with a specialization in Leadership. She has experience in project management, volunteer management, board relations, donor stewardship and event planning. Rose worked as a program manager at the Advancement and Alumni Relations department of Concordia University for 9 years. She graduated with a BComm' degree from the John Molson School of Business in 2006.

She is a wife and mother of one.

Rose is passionate about the work of God. She currently helps her husband, Pastor,Jean Yves Ntone, co-lead the Montreal West branch of Overcomers Assembly as well as lead the Communications department. During her spare time, she enjoys hosting friends and family, watching documentaries and keeping up with her etiquette blog titled, Etiquettehub.com.

She can be reached at Rose.Wangechi7@gmail.com

.†.

Secured in God's Perfect Love

By Esperance M Ntone Epee

I had the privilege of growing up in a family where both parents were born-again believers. Thanks to my parents, from the time I had an understanding of who God is, I knew that He was a loving God and that He loved me.

I had the privilege of growing up in a family where both parents were born-again believers. Thanks to my parents, from the time I had an understanding of who God is, I knew that He was a loving God and that He loved me.

My parents lived out their love of God–that is, their Christianity–in such an authentic way. It wasn't about rituals and tradition, nor was it about obligations and fear.

They loved God regardless of the circumstance they found themselves in. Whether there was lack or abundance, they loved Him and they lived for Him.

Like most children, one of the first verses that I memorized was John 3:16. It was only as a pre-teen, however, that I started having a little understanding of the loving sacrifice that God had done for the world, me included.

It was then that I made the conscious decision to have my own relationship with God. I remember telling Him that I was choosing to love and serve Him not as my parent's God, but as my own God. I recognized how in His love He had redeemed me, and I told Him that my life was His.

In my teen years, however, in my effort to *sustain* God's love, I tried to be a "good girl". I didn't do things that I shouldn't have anyways; not out of love or wanting to please my Saviour, but rather out of obligation and fear of losing out on His love for me.

This led up to a lot of frustrations and fears. When I would make a mistake and repent, I would doubt that He could easily forgive me. I would doubt my salvation as well. I'd try to win back his love by trying to be "better".

I, unfortunately, started to lead a work-based relationship with Him. I didn't realize this at the time, but I wasn't really satisfied in Him. How could I, when it was I who was at the center of my relationship with God? So when I failed in my own eyes, I was certainly not at peace. There were a lot of roller coaster moments. Deep down, I knew that this wasn't how it was supposed to be. I loved Him, but I knew that something wasn't right in our relationship.

It was only in my undergrad years, that I finally understood that God's love has nothing to do with us, and everything to do with Him. He doesn't love us because of what we've done or could ever do. He loves us because of His nature. He tells us that in His word that we love because He first loved us (1 John 4:19). I also understood that there was nothing that I could ever do that would make Him love me more. His love is perfectly perfect. There's nothing to add to it and nothing can be taken away from it.

There is a thought that often comes to mind; and when it does, it leaves me humbled.

It amazes me that God Almighty sees beyond the words that we speak and the actions that we take; into the thoughts that we think, and even beyond that, well into the motivations and intentions behind it all. I'm humbled that with this ongoing full knowledge that He has of us, and of me individually, He continues to love us.

Such knowledge can be terrifying, but it leaves me humbled and loving Him even the more. I can rest and be satisfied in His love for it is unchanging and does not rely on me.

Espérance M. Ntone Epée is a woman who lives to be fully satisfied in God. She loves God and wants others to experience the joy and life-changing impact of knowing Him.

She loves to write songs, fiction and nonfiction that makes much of God and brings people into a (deeper) relationship with Him. You can see more of her work at www.satisfiedingod.com

She currently resides in Montreal, with her husband and her son Noah, where she works as an RN in a Palliative Care Unit.

.†.

Daring On The Wings Of Love

By Bola Sobanjo

Summary statement: With God's love, you find strength to go beyond your fears

We know how much God loves us, and we have put our trust in his love. God is love, and all who live in love live in God, and God lives in them. 1 John 4:16(NLT)

Love personalized

Through the years, I have come to learn that our understanding and appreciation of love differs based on our personality, experiences and insights. Gary Chapman, a seasoned marriage counselor describes it as the five love languages[1]. Aside from his book on the subject, there are tools and tests which have been developed to help people identify how they express and receive love.

I remember when I was younger, in my teenage years. I was in a bad place. I struggled with acceptance. I needed to feel loved, valued. I was already a Christian then and so I spent a lot of time talking to God about my feelings and how I felt within. I remember asking Him to show me His love. Some days, overwhelmed with longing, I would ask for a hug and sure enough as I went into the day, someone would step up and give me a bear hug. Such a gesture would not have as much meaning to me now as it did then for two reasons: firstly, at that point in my life, I needed reassurance, I was looking for love whereas now, I'm much more secure in God's love and in the love of friends and family that surround me. The

---

[1] Gary Chapman. 2010. The 5 love languages: the secret to love that lasts.

other reason is linked to the cultural environment in which I grew up. It wasn't very common for parents and family members to be physically expressive. It was more culturally appropriate to give gifts, to meet the needs and to do things for loved ones than to cuddle and embrace them.

Now I no longer have to worry about being loved and accepted. Not only have I seen it express it in my life but I read it in His word. The bible tells us of God's love for us. I am told that God loved me enough to give His only beloved Jesus to die in my place (John 3:16). I am reminded of the great love God lavished on me that I might become His child (1 John 3:1). I matter to Him. He chose me.

Love emboldens

The knowledge of God's love for me makes me secure. It frees me from the need to constantly seek approval from others. It permits me to be me, the one whom God chose and in whom He delights.

"For the LORD your God is living among you. He is a mighty savior. He will take delight in you with gladness. With his love, he will calm all your fears. He will rejoice over you with joyful songs". Zephaniah 3:17

Knowing I am loved by God makes me realize that there is something special about me for me to be so loved. Seeing as God created me and knows me I am convinced that there are parts of me that I am yet to discover. I feel excited and seek constantly to bring that which is special in me into evidence. I want others to see it too. I realize I have something to offer and I want to share it with those around me. I want them to appreciate the handiwork of God. I walk tall with my head held high for I know that He is my glory and the lifter of my head (Psalm 3:3).

Love empowers

1 John 4:16 says, "We know how much God loves us and we have put our trust in His love".

That aptly describes where I am with God right now. Love encourages trust, trust in God's ability and in our self. It stimulates confidence. The fact that someone believes in us and is cheering us on, calling us out makes us want to go, to attempt things we otherwise would not have attempted.

When God called Moses to go lead His people out of Egypt, Moses was afraid, he doubted himself. He did not want to go, but when God reassured him with the display of His power and the promise of going with him, Moses accepted (Exodus 3). It is the same for us, knowing we are not alone also makes it possible. When people go scuba-diving or kite-boarding for the first time, it usually helps to have an experienced friend or instructor with them. It helps to know that you are not alone; to know that God is with you at all times (Heberews 13:6). God who is with us is all powerful and He loves us. He wants our best. He is rooting for us. He is not going to leave us alone, He will be with us through the dark places arranging hugs and cheers for us along the way (Isaiah 43:2).

Like Moses, we are often called to carry out tasks that seem beyond our capabilities. Such tasks might not seem as lofty as Moses' task was, but they challenge us nonetheless. For some, it is being a wife or a mother, you constantly find yourself out of depths, trying to keep it all together but afraid you will fail. For others, it might be a career path you feel called to take; it might involve serving others around you or even moving to a new city or country. Regardless of what the challenge looks like, one thing that is common to all is fear, self-doubt. The first instinct is to think like Moses', "I'm not cut out for this", "I cannot do this", "I am just plain old me". We ask God to find someone else better suited, someone more articulate, more intelligent.

The truth is God chose us. He chose me and He chose you. He made us. He knows us and He loves us. He wants the best for us at all times. He seeks to make the most of all that He has put in us and this is only possible if we are willing to trust Him. Love requires trust. Trust in the ability and intents of our beloved.

Moses had a speech impediment (Exodus 4:10) but it didn't stop God from using him. God can make the best use of our limitations and specializes in bringing beauty in the most unlikely places (Isaiah 61:3). Not only does His love & presence help to start the process, it helps to sustain the process. It is reassuring to know that it is His idea, He loves you and He is looking out for you all the way.

Love dispels fear

Does that mean there is no fear at all? No it does not. There will be fearful thoughts. Moses was afraid, so was Gideon and Mary (Exodus 4). Every time God has asked me to embark on a new project, I have felt the same. I start out worrying about how the possibilities of failure. The enemy feeds my mind with thoughts of fear: fear that my reputation would be tarnished, fear that I would fail and go into debt, fear that I would be made a laughing stock, fear of loneliness etc.

So what do I do with these fearful thoughts? How do I overcome them? How do I find the strength to go beyond my fears? I remember what I have just shared with you. I remember God loves me.

> *Such love has no fear, because perfect love expels all fear. If we are afraid, it is for fear of punishment, and this shows that we have not fully experienced his perfect love. 1 John 4:18 NLT*

I recall how faithful and unconditional His love is. I realize that God's intention in calling me out is not to punish me but to love me. So I take hold of every fearful thought and send it on its way, I refuse to dwell on it (2 Corinthians 10:5). That is the key to letting go and enjoying the journey. Refusing to give the enemy of your soul the privilege of depriving you of all God has in store for you.

Therefore..

Perfect love expels all fear...the fear of adventure, the fear of living unreservedly for what you believe, the fear of daring to take a stand, of getting your feet wet. God's love assures you that you have nothing to lose but everything to gain. It brings you into a place of trust that results in a deeper intimacy with the lover of your soul & that, is so worth it.

Bola Sobanjo is a woman committed to living out God's will for her life. Her commitment to God's call on her life has meant taking bold steps such as leaving behind a successful career in the UK to start over in Canada where she continues to delight in His love for her. Passionate about helping others grow in faith, she leads a life group and is also involved in the student outreach ministry of her local church. Bola is a family physician with public health expertise.

.†.

Living The Life Of Intentionality & Value

By Cynthia Egbunonu

To live intentionally is to deliberately do things that correspond to a person's value. It requires one to be **aware** of one's **fundamental beliefs** and be willing to make an effort to have their behavior reflect these beliefs in a form of integrity in relation to his or her conscience and environment.

Similarly, living a life of value is living a life of intentionality. One cannot live a life of value without being intentional in every area of the individual's life. I believe that living a life of value requires a person to desire and be intentional in consistently adding value to situations and people around them. The decision to live a life of value will help to direct the decisions we make on a daily basis. From a personal experience, I made a decision about a year ago to add value to people's lives and ever since that decision; I am constantly filtering my thoughts, actions and words with this value in my mind. I always ask myself how what I am doing adds value to the people and situations around me. I have noticed my thought pattern gradually change for the better as well as my words and actions towards people. I must say, it's been an amazing journey.

Living intentionally requires every action, word and thought be aligned to your desired destination. Like the GPS device which outlines the path to our desired destination. As soon as the destination is programmed into the device, the route from your starting point or current location to your destination is calculated by the device. As long as you follow the path outlined in the device, you will arrive at your expected destination. Since we are children of God, his Word (the bible) points us to the path he wants us to follow. Psalm 119:105 says, "Your word is a lamp to guide my feet and a light for my path." (NLT)

According to God's words, we ought to daily please God in every way by understanding what is pleasing to him. When we make the decision to please God everyday, we become intentional in our walk with him and as he reveals things to us, we are able to follow through with them knowing that they are for good.

> *"Don't copy the behavior and customs of this world, but let God transform you into a new person by changing the way you think. Then you will learn to know God's will for you, which is good and pleasing and perfect" – Romans 12:2 (NLT)*

> *"Then the way you live will always honor and please the Lord, and your lives will produce every kind of good fruit. All the while, you will grow as you learn to know God better and better" – Colossians 1:10 (NLT)*

"And try to learn [by experience] what is pleasing to the Lord [and letting your lifestyles be examples of what is most acceptable to Him—your behavior expressing gratitude to God for your salvation]" – Ephesians 5:10 (AMP)

Purpose (Calling)

Purpose is defined as the reason for which something is done or created or for which something exists. Have you ever reflected on questions such as these;

- What is my purpose here on earth?
- For what reason was I created?
- What have I been destined to accomplish?
- What goal or objective am I equipped to achieve?'

If you have, you are well on your way to living out that life of Intentionality and value. If you have never thought about them, today is a good day to start. When you get a new job or position in a company, you want to know and understand the reason why you were hired in order to align your goals, objectives, actions and results to the job requirements and expectations. The job profile or annual performance expectation document are also good references to compare your attitudes and outputs against while in the job. If this is not done, you may soon find yourself out of alignment and out of the job as a result. This is the same way we ought to understand our 'WHY- Purpose, calling'; we can't afford to continue to exist through life and depend on our day-to-day routines to get us through. And then the cycle continues. I believe that we are created for much more than existing through life. This is the reason we have the power to choose what we want. We may not have been able to choose our past but we can definitely create and choose our future experiences, opportunities and desired outcomes.

It starts within us, in our mind and inner self. When I started reflecting on the questions above, I wanted so much to understand who I am and what it is I am passionate about, this was important for me as I knew that I needed that information in order to discover my purpose. I also reflected on what I currently have (my abilities, attitudes, skills and talents), what I have acquired from my past (that which has made me the person I am today) - upbringing, experiences, opportunities, mistakes, learnings and the opportunities I have for growing and the person I can become in the future. During this process, I grew in my relationship with God my creator, my source for all things, the one who loves me with an everlasting love and who has great plans for my life. The one who will direct me in the way that I should go and will never leave me nor forsake me. Every moment I spend with God is so valuable as I went on this journey; I found my perspectives began to change gradually, my passion and desires became clearer. I became more open to understanding who I was in him, the way he saw me; I accepted his assessment of me. This new found knowledge increased my self confidence. Then I began to seek ways to equip myself for the journey and ask that my eyes be opened to understand the situations, opportunities and mistakes that may come my way. Truths that were not clear to me in the past became clearer. I am now daily making that conscious decision to pursue my purpose by being intentional in every area of my life while relying on God's grace every step of the way.

I believe that God has created each of us with a unique purpose and have instilled in us the ability to show forth his glory. I have never met or read about anybody who made a decision to add value and be intentional on a daily basis not excel in their area of interest. We have the innate ability to excel at anything we set our minds to and with the Holy spirit in us, we can accomplish even much more. When we live a life of intentionality, we choose to add value to our lives as well as the lives of other, as we experience growth and significance, our self confidence in increased. Every time we choose to do less than we could, this error in judgment has an effect on our self-confidence. Repeated every day, we soon find ourselves not only doing less than we should, but also being less than we could. The accumulative effect of this error in judgment can be devastating. I have come to understand that it is not enough to think positively; acting and speaking positively is what makes the difference.

Someone may say "I am content with living a good life, I don't need to be intentional" – That may be true however, is that your purpose in life? No individual accomplished significance without some level of intentionality. When we study the lives of accomplished individuals whether in the Christian or secular world, we see some level of intentionality in their attitude, passion and desires. And even better when we study the lives of those who were not only intentional but also sought to add value, they are the most significance accomplished people in the world. Long after they are gone, their lives continue to impact people for generations to come.

You can experience the best God has for you when you live a life of value and intentionality. Intentionality happens when you combine you thinking (information), your feeling (insight) and your doing (action). Gathering the facts you need to know about the situation – this is your thinking process. Looking at the situation in a new, heart-felt way. This insight often comes from Scripture; and doing something with the information and insight you've gathered. Without action, nothing happens. A balance of intentional Thinking, Feeling and Doing will result in an extraordinary life filled with peace, passion and progress. It is important to realize that I cannot give to others what I have not received. To extend God's love completely one must die to self-centeredness by reflecting the image of Christ. This begins by recognizing all your rights, goals, and identity was nailed to the cross. It's a process but one which will pay huge dividends.

I must also admit that living this kind of life does not come easily; we need some level of determination, discipline and consistency. As we make the decision and with the help of God's spirit in us, we gradually discover that there are certain things that we will focus more on or gravitate towards on a consistent basis and there are things that we will focus less on and pull away from. As you go through this process, do not forget to ask the holy spirit for help every step of the way. You may also begin to look for resources in your area of interest and passion to get you going on that path. Remember to filter your decisions through your 'why'. On this journey, you may also find that you become vulnerable and open to other people's judgment and actions. There will be some bumps along the way. With an open mind, we can learn through it all and as a result grow in our knowledge and wisdom and though the sacrifices may seem great, the benefits greatly outweigh the sacrifices.

I used to justify myself by asking, I always have very good intentions and I always think about the best for people, that should count right? I definitely agree with thinking positively and having good intentions for people and things around us, however, having good intentions is not enough. Unless actions are attached to the good intentions they remain that, good intentions. Have you heard the saying that the richest place in the world is the graveyards because in there lies great talents that were never tapped into, great passions that were never pursued and great purposes that were never fulfilled; Living a life of intentionality requires putting our good intentions into action. Leadership expert, John C Maxwell gives us sample words differentiating good intentions and intentional living.

Good intentions	**Intentional Living**
Hopefully	Definitive
Wish	Purpose
Desire	Action
Occasional	Continual
Emotion	Discipline
Passive	Active
Someday	Today
Survival	Success
Fantasy	Strategy
Somebody should	I will

Choose today to be a person of value and intentionality; choose to guard your thoughts, time, talents, passion and actions and channel them into fulfilling your purpose. Choose to add action daily to your good intentions.

About 15 years ago, I had a desire to see young girls become all that they can be, and that with exposure to the right resources, we could all accomplish much; however, over the last couple years, that desire has broadened as God has enlarged my perspective and horizon. I now desire to see people who can rise above their challenges, failures, hurts, pasts, adversities and do great things for God, themselves and their communities. I desire to see a world where people think of others before themselves and where adding value to others is a priority.

You are Unique

Cynthia is a practical and thoughtful leader with a sincere love for people and, a heart for God. She has a Bachelor's degree in Computer Sciene and Mathematics from Federal University of Technology Owerri, and, a Bachelor of Commerce degree from Laurentian University, Canada. Cynthia currently works as a Business Analyst at Empire Life.

Cynthia currently resides in Kingston, Ontario with her husband - Patrick Egbunonu- and their three childrem Samuel, Chioma, Amarachi. She and her husband currently lead the Kingston branch of OVercomers Assembly.

.†.

A Mother's Love

By Obaraboye Ine Olude

The word mother was first known to be used in the 12th century; referring to a female parent, one with maternal affection.

Descriptions of her could range from one who "gives birth to a child" to adoptive or stepmothers to mothering meaning "to watch over, nourish and protect maternally." With these definitions I want to put it to you that I am talking about every woman, since we all have the capacity to be a mother whether we have children or not.

A mother's love begins even before we are born and lasts for a lifetime. Luffina Lourduraj said,

'I don't believe in love at first sight because my mother started loving me before seeing me'. This is similar to what the Bible says in

Romans 5:8

'But God demonstrates His own love towards us, in that while we were still sinners, Christ died for us'. (NIV) (2)

That is, before we came to know God through Jesus Christ, God loved us. God has loved us from the beginning of time and gave a precious gift to us, His son Jesus to bring us back to himself after the fall. Thank God for his love for us. The Mother's relationship with her child is used in many scenarios in the scriptures.

For example, Prophet Isaiah used a mother's love to illustrate God's everlasting love for mankind with the illustration of a mother and her new baby.

Isaiah 49:15

The Lord answers, "Can a woman forget the baby she nurses?
Can she feel no kindness for the child she gave birth to?
Even if she could forget her children,
I will not forget you. (3)

Generally it is believed that a nursing mother is always close to her child to provide succor, comfort, care, food and love to her child. Isaiah mentions here that the love God has for us can be compared to that of a nursing mother; who though she loves much may forget her child. It is uncommon for her to forget she is nursing; And that could happen for a couple of reasons we wouldn't be highlighting here. However, God has promised, that even though there could be reasons why it may appear that a nursing mother forgets her child; he would never forget us. God's love is enduring and everlasting and so as mothers that have experienced God's love, it is easier for us to have such enduring love for our children.

Again, Paul compared the love he had for the believers in Thessalonica to that of a mother as in I Thessalonians 2:7-9. He describes the deep love and concern he had for the church. The church was established by Paul and the apostles that worked with him sometime in around AD49[6]. After the church was founded, Paul had to make another trip to visit another church and so didn't get to spend as much time as he would have loved to in order to build them up in faith.

While Paul was away he kept praying for them and asking after their welfare, while seeking opportunities to go back to visit them. When the opportunity came he sent Timothy a friend and brother to visit on his behalf and was glad with the report that he received back.1 Thessalonians 2:7-9

---

7 But we were very gentle with you. We were like a mother caring for her little children. 8 Because we loved you, we were happy to share God's Good News with you. But not only that, we were also happy

to share even our own lives with you. 9
Brothers, I know that you remember how hard we worked. We worked night and day so that we would not burden any of you while we preached God's Good News to you. (4)

In this passage ,Paul, compares the love he had for this church with that of a nursing mother for her child. Here is another opportunity to highlight the design in motherhood.

A few points to highlight about this love as mentioned in this passage are:

- Gentle. A mother is gentle with her child even through discipline and times of rebellion in a growing child, her love is tender and gentle.
- Caring - a mother cares genuinely for her child. It's a love that is expressed not based on it being reciprocated. Humans generally show love to or favour those who they know are able to help them in times of their own need. Mothers nurture and care no matter what.

As mothers, as we receive God's unconditional love, we must also learn to share this love with our children. The love a mother has for her child must move her to share her faith with them. I believe God has placed mother's especially to teach their children the word, teach them to pray, teach them to give. A child will reflect what he has learnt from his mother

The Bible in Proverbs 22:6 says

> *Train a child how to live the right way. Then even when he is old, he will still live that way. (7)*

I believe child upbringing is a call and that woman have been graced to do this well.. The failure of the society today can be partly linked to vices that were taught to children who then become the adult of tomorrow.

The life of God in us produces that like of it in others as we share with them. And it's never too early to begin to teach our children the word of

God, teach them to pray, let them see you pray, let them hear you worship, pray and give. These are seeds being sown in their lives and will yield its fruit in due season.

A popular Bible example of the faith of a mother being transferred to her child is seen in the story of Timothy; an apostle who worked with Paul. Paul recognized the faith in him and traced it back to his mother and grandmother.

2 Timothy 1:5

I remember your true faith. That kind of faith first belonged to your grandmother Lois and to your mother Eunice. And I know that you now have that same faith. (5)

A thought to consider as a mom, how much of your faith have you shared with your children. The greatest gift you can give your child is teaching them about God so that they have a personal relationship with Jesus. It brings such Joy and peace to you.

Eunice didn't just teach her faith to her son, she also taught him scriptures.

2 Timothy 3:14-17

> *14 But you should continue following the teachings that you learned. You know that these teachings are true. And you know you can trust those who taught you. 15 You have known the Holy Scriptures since you were a child. The Scriptures are able to make you wise. And that wisdom leads to salvation through faith in Christ Jesus. 16 All Scripture is inspired by God and is useful for teaching and for showing people what is wrong in their lives. It is useful for correcting faults and teaching how to live right. 17 Using the Scriptures, the person who serves God will be ready and will have everything he needs to do every good work. (8)*

He was taught the scriptures from a tender age, and was being encouraged to continue in them.

Prayers must go hand in hand as we share Christ's love with our children. We must do it with His help, praying for them, that through it all they will personally meet Christ and embrace him as their personal savior

I Thessalonians 3:10

10 And we continue praying with all our heart for you night and day. We pray that we can see you again and give you all the things you need to make your faith strong. (9)

There is much more we can do, I believe teaching a child doesn't just end at our faith and the word of God, some moms are blessed to home-school their kids. We can teach virtues, etiquettes, how to help out with chores at home, cooking..etc are a few important skills sets that a mom is privileged to inculcate in her child. I wouldn't forget the book by Stormie Omartian, "The power of a praying mom". The love she has for her kids and her family drives her to intercede for them daily and at all time.

- They shared their life with them

I remember a story I read a couple of years ago, I can't quite remember where I had read it from; would have loved to share with you right here.

It was shared by a man, who was the little boy in the story. He said he learnt giving from his mother. The story of a little boy who lived with his mom. They were not very rich but had a little to eat from the garden she had behind the house and bought other things with the little money she made. They lived in a pretty small house and didn't have the luxury of being fancy in their dressing.

A couple of days a week they had a stranger who always came knocking at their door just around dinner time asking for food for her kids. His mom would always find something to send her off with no matter how little. On some days, this little boy I believe about 6 years old, would be sent to get the door at the usual time when this "stranger" would come asking for food. His mom would hand him the food to go give to her. This practice became part of that little boy and when he became an adult, he found it easy to lend a helping hand and give to strangers. Mothers, let our love for our children move us to show them the right example.

There is no perfect mom, but Mom that have experience God's perfect love will daily receiver the Grace to pour out the same love to their children around them she could make mistakes and wrong choices but the enduring love comes to her aid to heal and to restore.

As a Christian mom I would encourage you to trust God more for grace to love more and more. God is the source of Love He is able to endow us with grace, strength and wisdom to use what he has deposited in us.

1 John 4:7-10

7 Dear friends, we should love each other,

*because love comes from God. The person who loves has become God's child and knows God. 8 whoever does not love does not know God, because God is love.
9 This is how God showed his love to us: He sent his only Son into the world to give us life through him. 10 True love is God's love for us, not our love for God. God sent his Son to die in our place to take away our sins. (10)*

I would like to conclude this chapter with a few quotes that speak of the love of a mother. I got them from my own mum Lady Cornelia.E.Derikoma. Who co-authored this chapter with me and encouraged me through till its completion. She is indeed an example.

God bless you mom!

Popular Quotes

- A mother always has to think twice, once for herself and once for her child (Sophia Loren)
- A mother is the truest friend we have. The tie which links mother and child is of such pure and immaculate strength as to be never violated (Washington Irving)
- A mother's love is patient and forgiving when all others are forsaking. It never fails or falters, even though the heart is breaking (Helen Steiner Rice)
- Life began with walking up and loving my mother's face (George Eliot)
- Mother-child relationship is paradoxical, and in a sense tragic. ... Mother's love is peace. It need not be acquired. It need not be deserved (Erich Fromm)
- There is no way to be a perfect mother, and a million ways to be a good one (Jill Church III)
- All that I am, or hope to be, I owe to my angel mother. I regard no man as poor who has a godly mother (Abraham Lincoln)

- I want my children to have all the things I couldn't afford. Then I want to move in with them (Phyllis Diller)
- Being a full-time mother is one of the highest salaried jobs ... since the payment is pure love (Mildred B. Vermont)
- Mother is the name of God in the lips and hearts of children (William Makepeace Thackeray)
- There is only one pretty child in the world, and every mother has it (Chinese Proverbs)

Obaraboye Ine Olude is a child of God. Got saved through the ministry of the Scripture Union Nigeria while in High school and has remained connected since. The wide variety of resources, camps and conferences gave her a solid foundation and strengthened her walk with God.

A trained Medical Doctor currently working in a Magnetic Resonance Imaging (MRI)-based neurological Research Company. Happily married to Gbolahan Olude and blessed with two wonderful boys Adedayo and Oluwatobi. She and her husband currently lead the Cote St Luc branch of Overcomers Assembly.

.†.

My Ephesians 5 Man

By Eguono Elena Onoyovwi

Pursued

She is his mission
the center of his focus
The object of his affection
His delightful pursuit

Refined

He is enthralled by her
Not only does he make a covenant of blessing with her
He commands everything around to bless her too
His business is to prepare the way for her
To sit as her purifier, he refines her
To make her shine like gold
To cover her in prayer
To wash her daily with the word

And present her as a beautiful bride
More precious than when they first met
With him by her side, she's confident
she will make heaven

Empowered

His job is tasking
His reward is with him
Mutual support is their guiding principle
"Babe look, I'll support you to become
the best of you even if it costs me all of me"
And her heart mirrors his
They are mutually empowered
Ignited by each other

Loved

She is his church
He loves her as Christ loved the church
and died for it
Daily he dies to himself
To his pride and ego
To his selfish ambition and thoughtless indifference
He is consistent
Through her ups and downs he remains
rooted in love
Even when his anger is aroused,
His overflowing love comes and quenches its fire

Because she is him - His own body

No one ever hates his own body, but
tenderly and lovingly cares for it
So there's no competition – he is
content with letting her shine

Sealed

He is her husband
Yes indeed! For many have masters but
hers is a husband

Her godly spouse
Her best friend for life
They can't be found apart
Like peas in a pod
They walk in tandem - Inseparable
And Christ is their seal

...

My Ephesians 5 man
I promise to not settle
I promise to wait for you
To trust and not waiver
So help me God

Help me God to understand, as all
God's people should, how wide, how long,
how high, and how deep your love is.

And if men can give good gifts to their children,
how much more you?
Yes, how much more!

Help me to realize that exceedingly
above my imagination your gift to me is
not just good but it's perfect

Like broken pieces that fit into each
other in multiple broken places
So two imperfect people bond into one
and 'Bone of my bone' is fulfilled

Help me to trust you completely

To know that even if you deny me my
eye candies and heart candies and
attention giving candies

Once, twice, three times and yet again

It's because you love me too much to let
me settle for less than your best

Help me to wait for this love like
the five wise virgins waited for the
bridegroom

I don't know at what hour he will come

But when he does may he find me

Emotionally available and spiritually
discerning
With my heart postured towards Christ
and none other

Yes help me God
For Pursued, Refined, Empowered,
Loved and Sealed I will be if I wait...

Yes, as I wait for my Ephesians 5 man <3

Eguono Elena Onoyovwi is a full-time tease from Nigeria. Ok on a serious note, she is a consultant with a background in business and engineering. She's passionate about youth having the right knowledge at the right time and consequently started a youth mentorship organization called New Culture. Her love for music and poetry led her to sing with church choirs, to learn to play the keyboard, and to launch a poetry hub at www.360Inspiration.ca.

Through her art, she hopes to convey the message that God really is madly in love with us, a truth that many still don't realize. Beyond that, Eguono is always up for a scrabble game and a road trip to anywhere serene with a promise of good food:)

.†.

God's Perfect Love Is Yours

As this book come to a close,

I pray that from his glorious, unlimited resources he will empower you with inner strength through his Spirit. Then Christ will make his home in your heart as you trust in him. Your root will grow down into God's love and keep you strong. And may you have the power to understand, as all God's people should, how wide, how long, how high, and how deep his love is. May you experience the love of Christ, though it is too great to understand fully. Then you will be made complete with all the fullness of life and power that comes from God.

That was Paul's prayer to the Ephesians and it is my prayers for you as well. I know that you desire to enjoy God fully, to have all fears destroyed. However, you may need to check if there is any obstacle on your way; Are you in the way? Your ideas, your fears, your limitations, your past, your present situation, your philosophy, your problems, even your achievements, your successes, your beliefs, your orientation, everything is yours and cant stand in your way.

You see, the God that made you and called you his own is God. He made all things and he knows all things. I am sure he has the blueprint of your life in his hands and is longing for you to surrender to him fully in order to fully enjoy your story.

You may even be like many, teaching the theory to others but the real experience of his love is far from you. You may have experienced him in the past, or you may have so much faith in His power. Whatever you story is, you need God's perfect love for life to be as it was designed to be.

Note that, your happily ever after story is definitely not going to be like any other's. So don't bother trying to compare. All I know is that your guide is your King and he is also the narrator of your story. He desires that you enjoy the story with him and he wants you to allow him carry you along some rocky roads.

Its doesn't matter what the devil says, it doesn't matter what some of your experiences reminds you of. All you need to know is that the mighty God is behind you like a mighty warrior. What then shall you fear?

God lavishes his love on us in Christ and His love is perfect. Mind you the word perfect does not mean flawless, but whole, complete. Same word as Jesus used at the cross when he said it is finished! Your anguish is finished and the ordeal is over. Christ your Messiah and King is here to reign in you.

God is love and Love is who God is. The DNA and attribute of God is love. Our new life in Christ has the same DNA. He pours his love on us and gives us the ability to pour it on others. That is why we are called beloved. Because we are beloved by him we can love like him. Remember its not a flawless love rather it's a whole love.

Christ love for us is complete. It cannot be added to. We are loved, we are his beloveds. And that's why John said we the beloved can easily love one another because we are full of love, his love has been made perfect in us.

Love is who God is.

When you have this love you naturally connect with others with the same love. When fear comes you will remember that you are his beloved. Choose to enjoy his love daily and as you do spread some of it to others around you.

I pray that you will recognize that the never tired advocate will always be there for you. Stand firm in his love and put on his whole armour, you will need every single one.

If you are reading this as a woman I must also add that the devil wants to get you down in order to get many others down like he did in Eve our dear mother. This is one more reason why you must stop to agree with the devil but start to fully pursue God.

The devil has not stopped and will not stop trying to get us down. However since we are beloved, we can chose to fight him back. Let's not allow him prevail. Stand firm in love. Put on love from the father and stand firm against the enemy.

God's love is for your protection

You are blessed!

.†.

ABOUT THE AUTHOR

Olu (Oluwaseun) Sobanjo is passionate about Christ. Working alongside her husband, Ade she serves as co-pastor at Overcomers Assemssbly since its inception in 2005. After planting 3 branches in different locations in Canada, Olu and her family are currently in Nigeria, planting a mission church in a community called Kuje, near Abuja, Nigeria; the Churches continues to be home for ordinary people living extraordinary lives.

She is mother to two wonderful boys (Demi & Damilola). Olu is a mentor and inspiration to women everywhere. She loves to help and see people pursue a thriving life in Christ.

Her desire to meet the needs of women led her to start the ladies ministry (single and married) at her church. She hosts the Vessels of Grace Conference (an annual ladies conference) since May of 2007.

She worked in financial planning for about 5 years until she left her practice in July 2012 to devote herself to full-time ministry. She enjoys pursuing Christ daily.

She helps people become all they were designed to be through her launchadream.com platform.

Other Books by Olu Sobanjo

In today's fast paced world, you can assume that doing certain spiritual activity regularly is what brings joy in Christ.

In this insightful book, Olu challenges readers to constantly look within in order to experience Christ's abundant life. She provides biblical insights and draws from her personal experience to illustrate how life in Christ can become richer and stronger.

Olu says; if you would make surrendering a part of your daily life you will start experiencing the unending joy of knowing Christ: thriving in life like Jesus; from the inside out.

It's high time the world sees the manifestations of the sons and daughters of God.

If you are ready to enter fully into your purpose in life through Christ, then you need to read this book.

Ade and Olu Sobanjo explain what you need to know and do to enjoy God grace that is available for you already. You can begin your work today.

Have you ever felt like God has forgotten you? You are not alone! Olu Sobanjo has created just the right tool that will boost your faith whenever you feel down and out. Weeping may last for the nights but joy comes in the morning. Be blessed

All available on Amazon or wherever books are sold.

www.ingramcontent.com/pod-product-compliance
Lightning Source LLC
Chambersburg PA
CBHW021129020426
42331CB00005B/684

* 9 7 8 0 9 7 8 1 5 9 5 8 0 *